Last Man

1

The Stranger

Balak + Sanlaville + Vivès

TIGHTEN YOUR STANCE.
STAY FOCUSED.

STAY LOOSE...
YES, LOOK FOR OPENINGS AND STRIKE!
SHHH
NEXT UP!
THOSE WHO WIN STAY ON...
THOSE WHO LOSE STAND DOWN.

I SAID STAY LOOSE!
RESPECT YOUR PARTNER, KIDS.
TAP
SHH
BAMF
TAP

GREGORIO, LOWER YOUR GUARD.
SHH-
BLAM

DID YOU SEE WHAT HAPPENED THERE?
EVEN WITH HIS GUARD DOWN, GREGORIO EASILY DEFLECTED ADRIAN'S ATTACK.
WHEN YOU ATTACK, ALWAYS ANTICIPATE YOUR OPPONENT'S REACTION! ALWAYS!
ADRIAN, YOU'D BETTER FIX THAT BEFORE THE TOURNAMENT. THAT GOES FOR ALL OF YOU, TOO.
OKAY, CLASS DISMISSED. DON'T FORGET TO SALUTE.
YES, SIR!
ADRIAN.
YOU OKAY?
YOU KNOW, THE MASTER WAS JUST MAKING A POINT.
IT WASN'T PERSONAL.
I KNOW.

WHO'S YOUR TEAMMATE?

IT'S VLAD. HE WAS THE ONLY ONE LEFT.
OH.

ONE BIT OF ADVICE? DON'T LET HIM EAT BEFORE THE FIGHT. WE WERE ON A TEAM ONCE, AND HE GOT SICK. SO...

ADRIAN, WANNA EAT AT MY HOUSE? MY MOM'S MAKING SEAFOOD GUMBO.

YOU COMING, ADRIAN?
SO HOW'D IT GO TODAY?
DID YOU GUYS PREP FOR THE TOURNAMENT?
...
CAT GOT YOUR TONGUE?

CLASS DIDN'T GO WELL?
ADRIAN.
HOW'D YOU LIKE SOME CHOCOLATE BREAD?
...AND THEN THE MASTER PICKED THE TEAMS.
SO WHO ARE YOU WITH?
VLAD.
HE'S SMALL, LIKE ME.

YOU KNOW WHAT, MOM?
WHAT?
I'M GONNA PRACTICE HARD TONIGHT— I WROTE DOWN A BUNCH OF MOVES.
THAT'S FINE, HONEY, BUT LET'S HAVE DINNER FIRST AND SEE AFTER THAT.
HHHSSSSSS
STOP, ONI!
HA HA!
HA HA!
ADRIAN, LEAVE ONI ALONE AND COME EAT.
TAC-

IT'S SO GOOD!
IT'S CANTALOUPE SALAD. I WAS WALKING THROUGH THE MARKET AND THOUGHT YOU'D LIKE IT.
YOU'RE NOT EATING?
NO, I HAD A BITE AT WORK.
YOU KNOW WHAT, MOM?
TELL ME.
EVEN IF MY PARTNER'S NOT THAT GOOD, WE'LL STILL WIN THE TOURNAMENT, I PROMISE!
THEN WE'LL GET THE BIG CUP FILLED WITH GOLD COINS AND WE CAN GO TO THE MARKET AND BUY ALL THE FOOD WE NEED.
FOREVER.

LOOK WHO WANTS TO HELP HIS POOR MOM!
BUT WE'RE DOING PRETTY WELL, YOU AND ME, DON'T YOU THINK?
YUP.
SO TOMORROW, DON'T THINK ABOUT ME. YOU'RE THERE TO HAVE FUN, REMEMBER THAT.
FOR NOW, YOU NEED TO REST UP FOR THE MORNING.

WHAM!
WHAM!
FEINT.
FIST LUNGE.
WHAM!
WHAM!
WHAM!

ROUNDHOUSE KICK!
WHAM!

GUARD UP.

YAAAAA!

ADRIAN! I SAID GET TO BED!

DOM DOM DOM DOM DOM
DOM DOM DOM DOM DOM
DOM-DOM-DOM-DOM

YOU GONNA BARF?

WHAT'S GOING ON?

DID HE BARF?

IT'S VLAD.

HE'S GONNA BARF.

LAY OFF IT, KIDS! YOU'LL ONLY MAKE HIM FEEL WORSE.

BUT IT'S VLAD. HE ALWAYS THROWS UP.

OKAY, LISTEN.

YOU'D BETTER NOT BE FAKING, BECAUSE THIS MEANS YOU AND YOUR TEAMMATE ARE OUT.

MY BELLY HURTS.

VLAD, LOOK AT ME. ARE YOU FAKING, OR WHAT?

GONNA THROW UP...

WELL...
...I'M AFRAID VLAD WON'T BE IN THE TOURNAMENT.
ADRIAN...
I'M SORRY.
TOO BAD, ADRIAN.
YOU NO LONGER HAVE A PARTNER...
AND THERE'S NO ONE ELSE...
SO YOU CAN'T BE IN THE TOURNAMENT THIS YEAR.

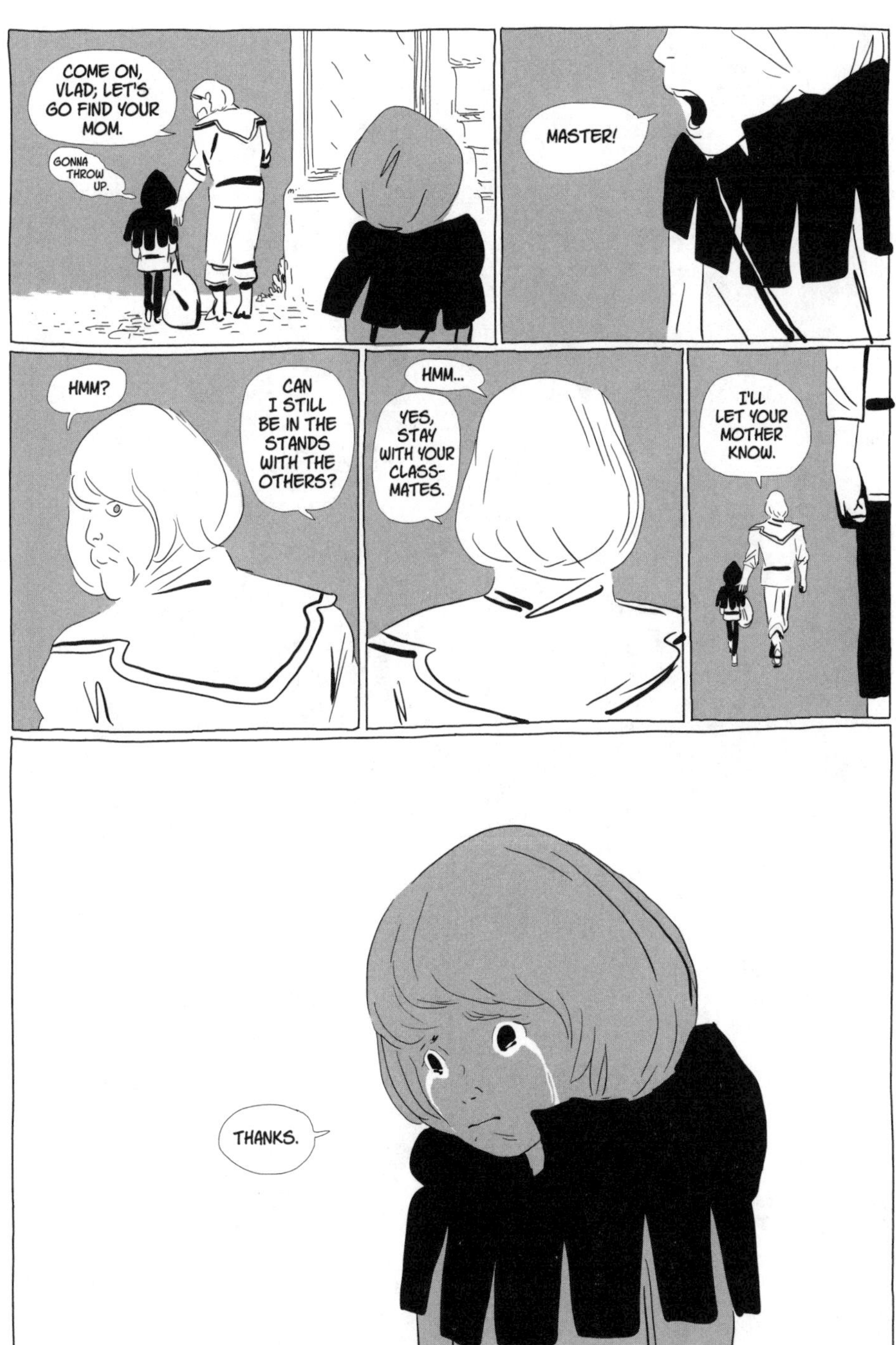
COME ON, VLAD; LET'S GO FIND YOUR MOM.
GONNA THROW UP.
MASTER!
HMM?
CAN I STILL BE IN THE STANDS WITH THE OTHERS?
HMM...
YES, STAY WITH YOUR CLASS-MATES.
I'LL LET YOUR MOTHER KNOW.
THANKS.

ANYTHING ELSE?
TWO LOAVES, ONE BRAID.
SEND IN THE MINCE PIES!
COMING THROUGH!
COMING THROUGH!
GULP!
MRS. VELBA!
MR. JANSEN? DID SOMETHING HAPPEN TO ADRIAN?
IT'S A PLEASURE TO SEE YOU, AND I DO APOLOGIZE FOR INTERRUPTING YOUR TASKS...
WHAT'S WRONG? IS HE HURT?
WELL, NO. BUT HIS PARTNER'S SICK, SO HE CAN'T...
OH NO!
BOSS, I GOTTA GO! EMERGENCY.
ALSO, I HAD BEEN MEANING TO ASK IF YOU GOT THAT NOTE I SENT?
OKAY, MARIANNE. NO PROBLEM.

THAT IS THE WORST THING THAT COULD'VE HAPPENED!

HE'S BEEN TALKING NON-STOP ABOUT THE TOURNAMENT.
HIS FIRST SHOT AT IT!
I CAN IMAGINE.

ADRIAN.

I HEARD.

ANOTHER PARTNER COULD TURN UP.
FAT CHANCE.

HONEST— DON'T GIVE UP YET!

ELO, YOU COMING?
WAIT A SEC. ADRIAN CAN'T COMPETE.
YEAH, I KNOW. THAT SUCKS.

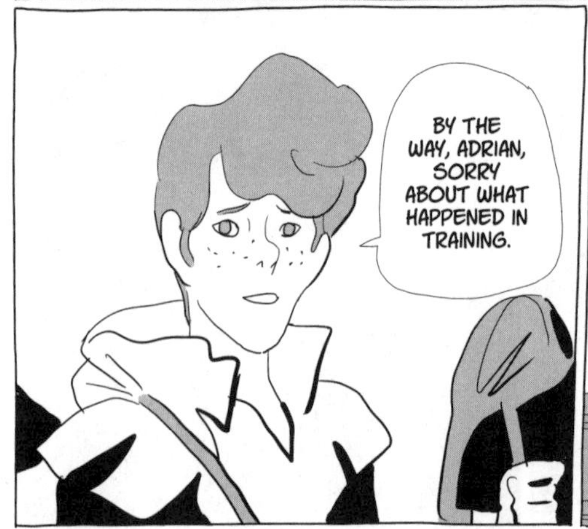
BY THE WAY, ADRIAN, SORRY ABOUT WHAT HAPPENED IN TRAINING.

IT'S OKAY, GREGORIO. YOU'RE BETTER THAN ME, ANYWAY.

DON'T SAY STUFF LIKE THAT.
ADRIAN.
COME ON, LET'S SIT SOMEWHERE.
NO!

FINE THEN. WE CAN TALK HERE. I'M LISTENING.
VLAD ATE SEAFOOD, AND NOW I CAN'T COMPETE!
IT'S A STROKE OF BAD LUCK, SWEETIE, BUT YOU HAVE TO LEARN TO TAKE STUFF LIKE THAT IN STRIDE.
LET'S GO TO REGISTRATION AND HOPE SOMEONE SHOWS UP. OKAY?
OKAY...
DOM
YOUR ATTENTION PLEASE...
DOM

DOM
REGISTRATION WILL CLOSE IN 30 MINUTES!
DOM

DOM
DOM
DOM
DOM
DOM
DOM...

MMM...

AH, MAN.
KRRK
SHHHHHHHHHHHHHHHHHHHHHHHHHHHHHHHHHHHHHHHH

SHH
DOM
DOM
DOM
DOM
DOM
DOM
DOM
DOM

WHAT THE HELL'S THAT RACKET?
NOW I'LL BE ZONKED FOR THE...
MORON!

DAMNDAMNDAMNDAMNDAMN
DAMN!

WHERE THE HELL IS IT?
AH!
SHH
EXCUSE ME!
...
HELLO, MA'AM. COULD YOU PLEASE TELL ME WHERE THE BIG TOURNAMENT IS?

...OKAY, AND DO YOU KNOW WHERE I CAN GET SOME SMOKES?

HEY!
CI-GA-RETTES!
FOR SMOKING!

DO YOU EVEN GET A WORD I'M SAYING?

OKAY, SCREW IT...

DOM
DOM
DOM
DOM
DOM

REGISTRATION IS UP THAT WAY!

AND WHERE CAN I FIND CIGARETTES?
?

WHAT THE HELL KIND OF TOWN IS THIS?

YOO-HOO!

WATCH WHERE YOU'RE GOING, KID.

GRRR!

C'MON! WE GOTTA FIND A GOOD SPOT!

HELLO, I'D LIKE TO REGISTER FOR THE TOURNAMENT.

SO SORRY— REGISTRATION CLOSED 10 MINUTES AGO.

OKAY, LET'S TRY THAT AGAIN.
HELLO, I'D LIKE TO REGISTER FOR THE TOURNAMENT.

LOOK, I'M SORRY, BUT THE SIGN-UP IS OVER. THE LIST OF PARTICIPANTS IS ABOUT TO BE SENT TO THE KING AND QUEEN.

YOU'RE TELLING ME I RACKED UP 1,000 MILES ON MY BIKE FOR NOTHING?

WHAT'S *"ON MY BIKE"*?
I DON'T GET IT.
I HAVE NO IDEA!

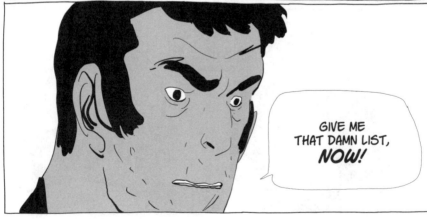

GIVE ME THAT DAMN LIST, ***NOW!***

OKAY, SO MY NAME GOES THERE...
AND HERE'S WHERE I SIGN?

HE HAS THE LIST.

PARTNER?!
WAIT—IT'S A TEAM COMPETITION?!

SERIOUSLY?
IT'S TRADITION.

TELL YOU WHAT. I'LL JUST WRITE MY NAME TWICE, AND WE'RE GOOD.
A PARTNER WOULD BE USELESS ANYWAY.

AGAIN, WE'RE TERRIBLY SORRY, BUT IT CAN'T BE DONE. THE WAY THE BOUTS ARE SET UP...
BUT I'M GONNA WHIP THEM ALL.
I DO UNDERSTAND, BUT NO ONE CAN REGISTER WITHOUT A PARTNER.
ALL RIGHT...
LET ME THINK.
YOU CAN'T BE SERIOUS—TEAM FIGHTS SUCK!
IT'S OKAY, ADRIAN...
NEXT YEAR YOU'LL GET A BETTER PARTNER AND HAVE A REAL SHOT AT WINNING THE CUP. IT'S NOT YOUR FAULT VLAD QUIT.

HMM...

OKAY, DUDES, IT'S ALL GOOD. BE BACK IN A FLASH.

WHAT DID HE MEAN, *"BACK IN A FLASH"*?
I HAVE NO IDEA.
WAIT, WHERE'S THE SIGN-UP SHEET?

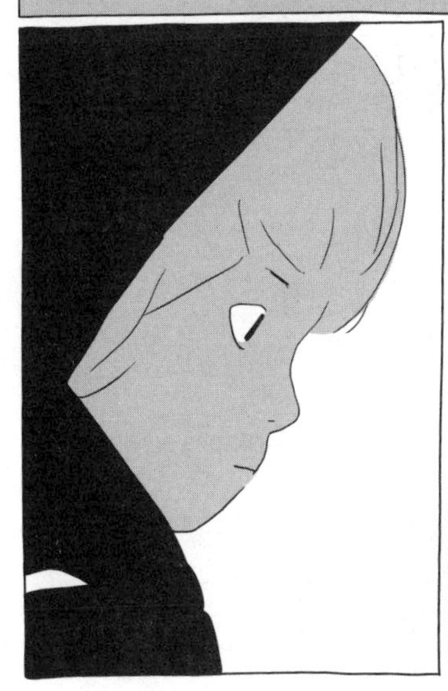

HEY, KID!

TELL ME...
DO YOU KNOW WHERE THAT BIG TOURNAMENT'S HAPPENING?
'CAUSE I'M WAITING FOR MY PARTNER. WE WERE SUPPOSED TO MEET UP HERE...
...BUT THERE'S NO SIGN OF HIM.

IT'S HERE.
OKAY, COOL.

LOOKS LIKE HE'S A NO-SHOW.
DON'T KNOW WHY I'M EVEN SURPRISED...
HE'S DONE IT BEFORE.

I WAS REALLY LOOKING FORWARD TO COMPETING...

GUESS I'LL HAVE TO FIND A NEW PARTNER.

OTHERWISE I'LL JUST HAVE TO GO HOME...

MMM...

WAIT!

I DON'T HAVE ANYONE EITHER! WE COULD TEAM UP!

TEAM UP? YOU AND ME?
HOW DO I KNOW YOU'RE ANY GOOD?

LISTEN, MISTER! THIS YEAR I TRAINED FOR THE TOURNAMENT WITH THE BIG KIDS, AND I KNOW ALL THE MOVES.

AND IF I WIN, WE'LL BE FAMOUS AND AT THE MARKET, THEY'LL GIVE US ALL THE FOOD WE CAN EAT.

WELL, KID, YOU SURE SEEM MOTIVATED.

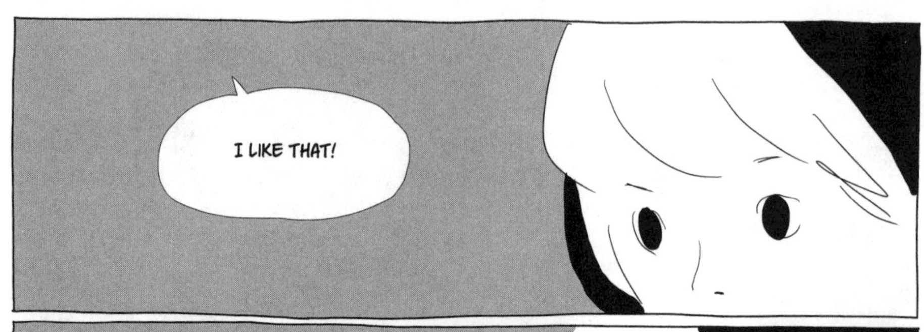

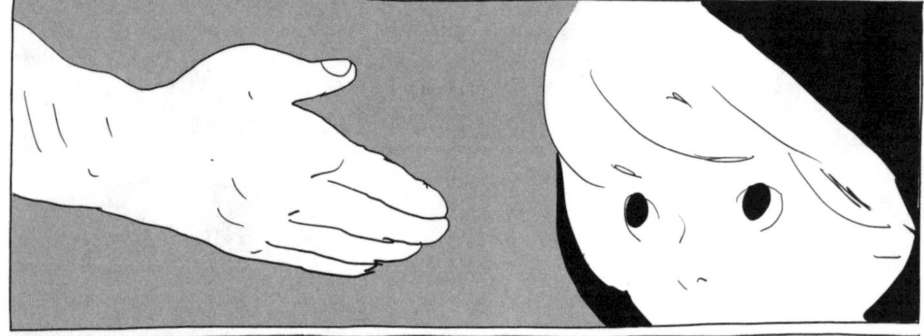

NAME'S RICHARD ALDANA.

AND YOU?

I'M ADRIAN VELBA, SIR.
PLEASED TO MEET YOU, ADRIAN.

BUT HOW CAN WE BE IN THE TOURNAMENT? REGISTRATION'S OVER.
NOT QUITE...

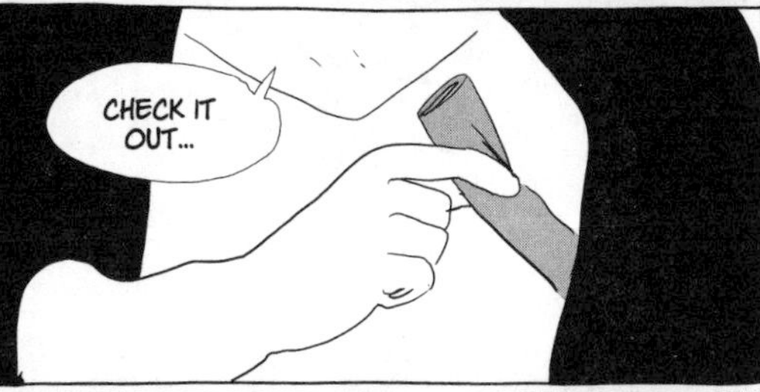

CHECK IT OUT...

ADRIAN?

MOM! GUESS WHAT?!
I FOUND A PARTNER.
HIS NAME'S RICHARD ALDANA.
HE WAS ALONE TOO!
YOU'RE ADRIAN'S MOM? IT'S A PLEASURE.
ADRIAN SEEMS LIKE A GOOD KID.

LET'S GO, ADRIAN.

BUT...
MOM?
THE TOURNAMENT.
WHY ARE WE LEAVING?
DON'T ARGUE, ADRIAN!
BUT I FOUND A PARTNER!

ADRIAN.
WHAT HAVE I TOLD YOU A THOUSAND TIMES ABOUT STRANGERS?
...
DON'T TALK TO THEM.
EXACTLY!
ESPECIALLY IF THEY MAKE WEIRD OFFERS LIKE THAT.
YOU HAVE NO IDEA WHAT COULD HAPPEN!
CRAP.

DAMN.
THINK, MAN...
ADRIAN!

SHH
TAP

I THINK THERE'S BEEN A MISUNDERSTANDING.

MA'AM, PLEASE KNOW THAT MY INTENTIONS ARE HONORABLE. I ONLY WANT TO COMPETE IN THE TOURNAMENT!

WOW... HE'S REALLY GOOD!
ALL RIGHT.
AND YOUR NAME IS...?
RICHARD ALDANA.
NEVER HEARD OF YOU.

MAKES SENSE. AFTER I WIN THE TOURNAMENT, YOU WILL.
WHERE ARE YOU FROM?
NO PLACE YOU'D KNOW.
I DOUBT IT; I KNOW EVERYONE AROUND HERE. AND I'VE NEVER BUMPED INTO YOU.
FATE MUST'VE WANTED US TO MEET TODAY.
VERY FUNNY. AND WHY TEAM UP WITH A 12-YEAR-OLD?
LIKE HIM, I DON'T WANT TO WAIT ANOTHER YEAR.
BUT WHY DOES THAT TOURNAMENT MEAN SO MUCH TO YOU?
I HAVE MY REASONS.

YOUR REASONS? WELL, LET'S HEAR THEM.
COME ON, MOM— STOP.

IT'S OKAY, ADRIAN.
I CAN'T BLAME HER.

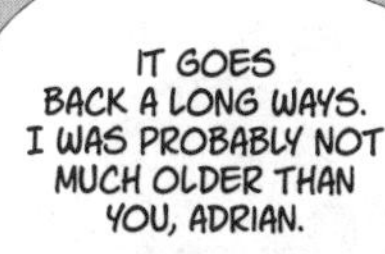
IT GOES BACK A LONG WAYS. I WAS PROBABLY NOT MUCH OLDER THAN YOU, ADRIAN.

IT WAS JUST THE TWO OF US, BEST FRIENDS PRACTICING MARTIAL ARTS.
WE WERE INSEPARABLE, SPENT ALL OUR TIME TRAINING.
PEOPLE EVEN NICKNAMED US *"THE KARATE BROTHERS."*

THEN WE GOT OLDER, AND WE WERE READY FOR OUR FIRST TOURNAMENT.
FATE DECIDED THAT MY FRIEND WOULD FIGHT THAI BOY, THE REIGNING CHAMPION.
FATE ALSO DECIDED THAT, IN THE SECOND ROUND OF A HEROIC FIGHT, MY FRIEND WOULD BE DEALT A DEADLY BLOW TO THE FACE.
HK!
I WAS BY HIS SIDE WHILE HE LAY ON THE GROUND, GLASSY EYES STARING AHEAD AS THAI BOY LAUGHED MERCILESSLY.
HIS LAST WORDS WERE, *"AVENGE ME, BROTHER... AVENGE ME!"*

SINCE THEN, I—
WHAT?! YOU THINK THAT STORY'S GOING TO CONVINCE ME TO LET YOU COMPETE WITH MY SON?!
MOM!
LOOK, I'M SORRY ABOUT YOUR KARATE FRIEND, BUT YOU HAVE TO UNDERSTAND...

ADRIAN IS THERE TO HAVE FUN, AND—

BUT MOM! IT WASN'T HIS FAULT—IT WAS THAI BOY'S!

PLEASE...

!
OKAY, MR. ALDANA.
I HAVE MY EYE ON YOU!

MR. JANSEN...

MR. JANSEN, THERE'S BEEN A SLIGHT CHANGE.
TURNS OUT ADRIAN FOUND A PARTNER.
HIS NAME'S RICHARD ALDANA.
SORRY FOR THE SHORT NOTICE—IT JUST HAPPENED.
I HOPE THIS WON'T BE TOO MUCH TROUBLE.
UM...NO... NOT AT ALL...

THIS IS AWESOME! I'M GONNA COMPETE IN MY FIRST TOURNAMENT!
HMM...
TELL ME, MISTER...
ALDANA.
ALDANA...
WHAT IS YOUR STYLE?
...
MY STYLE?
CERTAINLY YOU KNOW THAT EACH FIGHTER MUST HAVE MASTERED ONE OF THE ANCESTRAL STYLES.
HMM...
WHY SHOULD I TELL YOU? WHY DON'T YOU TELL ME YOURS?

MY STYLE?
...OOOOO
OOOOOH...
SHAIII!
SHH
SCHH
TAP

BLAC
YOU COULD'VE JUST TOLD ME.

GNNN...
YOU HAVE GOOD REFLEXES.
ANY TROUBLE, GENTLEMEN?
OH NO, NOTHING IMPORTANT, YOUR HOLINESS.
A LITTLE WARM-UP...
DO THAT AGAIN, ALDANA, AND I'LL—
BUT I'M NOT THE ONE WHO...
I WAS MERELY CHECKING. MAY THE GODS BRING YOU LUCK, TO YOU AND YOUR SCHOOL.

YOUR HOLINESS.
ADRIAN.
LISTEN CAREFULLY. WATCH YOUR STANCE, AND REMEMBER— KEEP YOUR GUARD UP. THEN YOU ATTACK. UNDERSTOOD?
YES, MASTER.

YOU'VE ALREADY FOUGHT HERE BEFORE?
UM, YEAH, SURE. I JUST DON'T REMEMBER THE RULES TOO WELL.
I KNOW 'EM BY HEART. I'LL TELL YOU.
I MUST ATTEND TO MY...STUDENT...
PARDON ME.
MR. JANSEN.
ONE MOMENT.

LISTEN, I'VE THOUGHT ABOUT YOUR NOTE AND YOUR INVITATION TO DINNER.
...

I'D BE GLAD TO GO.
I'M FREE TUESDAY.
WOULD THAT WORK?

SORRY, I HAVE TO RUN BACK TO THE OVEN.
HAVE A GOOD TOURNAMENT, MR. JANSEN.

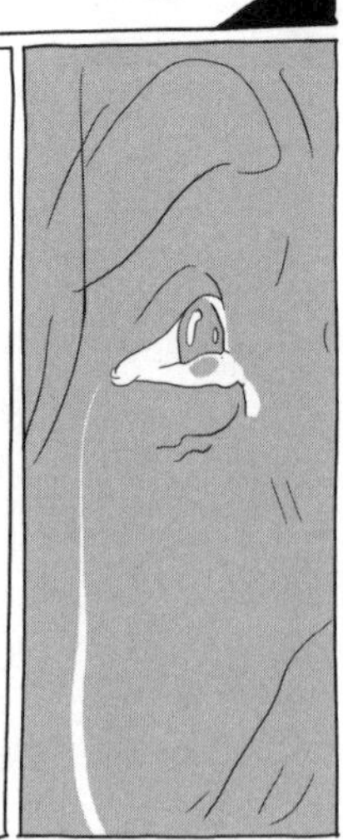

MASTER, OUR FIGHT IS ABOUT TO START.
COULD I GET YOUR TAKE ON A STRATEGY I THOUGHT OF?
CHILDREN...
THIS IS THE BEST DAY OF MY LIFE.
YOU FIGURE IT OUT.
BUT THAT'S INSANE!

WHY'D HE STOP THERE?!
TO START THE ENGAGEMENT, OF COURSE.

IF YOU SAY SO.

AND WHO'S HE, AGAIN?
DUH, THAT'S THE REFEREE.
YEAH, OF COURSE I KNEW THAT—JUST CHECKING.

BUT WHO'S THAT?
OH, THAT'S GREGORIO. HE'S THE BEST IN OUR SCHOOL.

LAST YEAR, HE GOT TO THE THIRD ROUND. NO OTHER KID'S EVER GOTTEN THAT FAR.

AND WHO'S THAT?
HE'S A STUDENT FROM THE AIR SCHOOL.
HE CAN DO WIND ATTACKS.
RIGHT. SO I'VE ENDED UP WITH MAGICIANS AGAIN...
HUH?
NEVER MIND.
AND YOU DO MAGIC TOO? PILLARS OF FIRE AND ALL THAT STUFF?
UM...
I'M STILL NOT THAT GREAT AT IT, BUT I CAN ALMOST DO EARTHQUAKES.
OKAY...NOW WHAT'S THAT GUY'S PROBLEM?
HE'S STARTING THE ENGAGEMENT, SENDING A WIND BLAST.
...

TAH
WOW—HE'S SUMMONING A LOT OF ENERGY.
WOOSH

BLOC
SHHH
OOOOOF!
TAP

YOUR CHAMPION LOOKS KINDA SHAKY.
HE HAS TO STAY ON HIS FEET.
BAH!
NO!
GREGORIO!
RING OUT!
THIS CAN'T BE HAPPENING!
DON'T TALK TO ME, ELORNA.
AND WHO'S SHE?
THAT'S ELORNA, HIS PARTNER.
...SHE'S NOT AS GOOD AS GREGORIO.

SHE HASN'T MASTERED ANY SPECIAL ATTACKS.

GOOD GUARD.

HE'S GEARING UP FOR ANOTHER WIND BLAST.

WOOSH

ELORNA'S DAD IS ONE OF THE GREATEST CHAMPIONS THE TOURNAMENT'S SEEN.
AND HE'S COMPETING?

NO, NOT ANYMORE.
EVEN WHEN I WAS LITTLE, HE'D ALREADY RETIRED.

SHE'S BEARING UP PRETTY WELL, YOU KNOW.

HER DAD CREATED LOTS OF COMBAT MOVES. HE RAN OUR SCHOOL BEFORE MASTER JANSEN.

HANG ON A SEC.

SHH
TAH—

TAP
SHH
BLAM

IMPRESSIVE FOR A GIRL HER AGE.
THEY'RE TALLYING THE SCORE.

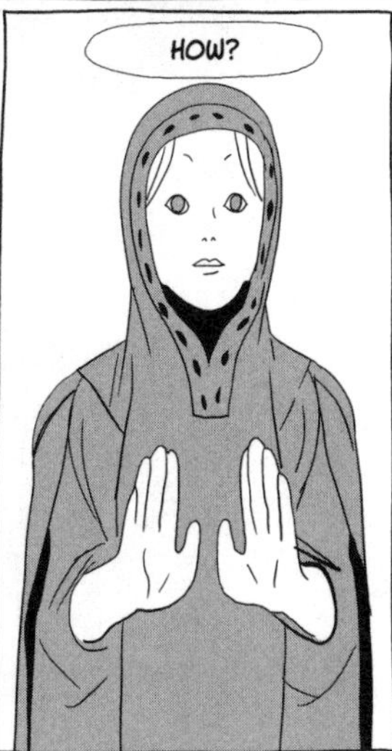
HOW?

COUNTER-ATTACK: -2.
BLOCKING ADVANTAGE: -1.
CONTACT: 3

HEY, SHE'S A HAND AHEAD. SHE'S GONNA WIN HER FIGHT.
HMM.

GROUND COMBINATION: -2.
VICTORY TO ELORNA MORGAN.
SECOND FIGHTER FROM THE OAK SCHOOL!

IF SHE CAN DO IT AGAIN...
TAK
OOH, RING OUT! THEY'RE SWEEPING THE FIRST ROUND!
YOU KNOW, BEFORE WE START THE TOURNAMENT, I'VE GOTTA ASK YOU SOMETHING.
WHAT'S THAT?
YOU KNOW YOUR MOM'S A BOMBSHELL, RIGHT?
BOMBSHELL?
YEAH, I GUESS YOU'RE USED TO IT...
BUT SHE'S REALLY SOME-THING.

Adrian Velba
Richard Aldana
ADRIAN VELBA...
Bert Flora
HE'S A KID, RIGHT?
Adrian Velba
Richard Aldana
B. Soares
J. Soares
AND THE OTHER?
RICHARD ALDANA.
QUALIFICATION
NEVER HEARD OF HIM.
WE SHOULD BE GOOD FOR THE FIRST ROUND.
A CAKEWALK.

ELORNA!

IF THEY HADN'T LET THAT STUPID BEGINNER GET AWAY WITH FOULING...
ADRIAN.

WOW, I SAW YOUR FIGHT—YOU WERE AMAZING!

CONGRATS FOR QUALIFYING, GREGORIO.

WILL YOU SHUT THE HELL UP?

DON'T YOU HAVE ANY FRIENDS?
GET OUTTA HERE!

ARE YOU OUT OF YOUR MIND TALKING LIKE THAT? APOLOGIZE RIGHT NOW!

HEY, JUST 'CAUSE YOU WON SOME SORRY-ASS FIGHT DOESN'T MEAN YOU CAN BOSS ME AROUND!

WHAT'RE YOU GONNA DO NOW, CRY?

YEAH, THAT'S RIGHT, GET THE HELL OUTTA HERE!

JUST DON'T FORGET WE STILL HAVE SOME FIGHTS COMIN' UP.

SO THOSE ARE OUR OPPONENTS...

CLEARLY A TEAM FROM THE REJECT PILE, THROWN TOGETHER AT THE LAST MINUTE.
GREAT FOR A WARM-UP.

WHO ARE THEY?
HEE HEE HEE...
WE ARE THE SOARES BROTHERS. IT'S A PLEASURE TO MEET YOU, DEAR OPPONENTS.
WE ARE HERE TO WIN. THAT EXOTIC LITTLE PAIRING OF YOURS IS AMUSING, BUT DON'T EXPECT ANY MERCY.
CAN'T HELP WONDERING IF YOUR TEAM WAS MEANT AS SOME KIND OF A JOKE.

I HOPE YOU'RE NOT EXPECTING TO MEASURE UP TO US.
HEE HEE...
LISTEN, CLOWNS. I'M GONNA MAKE A TRASH HEAP OUTTA YOU. GOT THAT?
THINK WE'RE IMPRESSED, STRANGER?

GENTLEMEN.
YOUR FIGHT STARTS IN 10 MINUTES, NOT BEFORE. MAT 7.
DON'T BE LATE.
HEE HEE.
OH NO, WE WON'T BE LATE.
HEE HEE.
MORONS.

WE'RE GONNA TEACH THOSE TWO BALLERINAS A LESSON.
READY, ADRIAN?
YES!

FIRST QUALIFYING ROUND.

TEAM SOARES
VERSUS
TEAM VELBA-ALDANA.
GENTLEMEN. HANDS TOGETHER.

LORD OF THE WORLDS, LEAD US TO THE TRUE PATH.

LEAD US TO THE TRUE PATH.
LEAD US TO THE TRUE PATH.
LEAD US TO THE TRUE PATH.
FROM YOUR COMPASSIO WAY TO ETERNAL SALVATION...
BLAH BLAH BLA BLAH BLAH BLAH...

GENTLEMEN, TO YOUR CORNERS.

MMHMHH...
MMHHHM...

WHY DID I HAVE TO END UP WITH FREAKIN' MAGICIANS?

RICHARD...

MASTER JANSEN TAUGHT US SOME SECRET MOVES.
I PRACTICED THEM FOR THE TOURNAMENT. I'M SURE I CAN BEAT AT LEAST ONE OF THESE GUYS.

REALLY?
OKAY, YOU'RE ON. YOU'LL GO FIRST.

YOU GO UP THERE, YOU DO YOUR SECRET MOVES, AND YOU TAKE THEM OUT FOR ME, OKAY?

FIRST FIGHTER, STEP FORWARD.

STAY FOCUSED, ADRIAN.
MAXIMUM FOCUS!

SHAI! SHAI! SHAI!

OKAY, LET'S SEE WHAT THE KID'S MADE OF.

TIME FOR A SMALL MIRACLE.

GENTLEMEN...
GET READY...
TEAM CHERONE AND TEAM AMBROSE QUALIFIED.
TEAM EDO ELIMINATED.
TEAM TIGER IN THE 2ND ROUND.
C'MON, ADRIAN.
FIGHT!

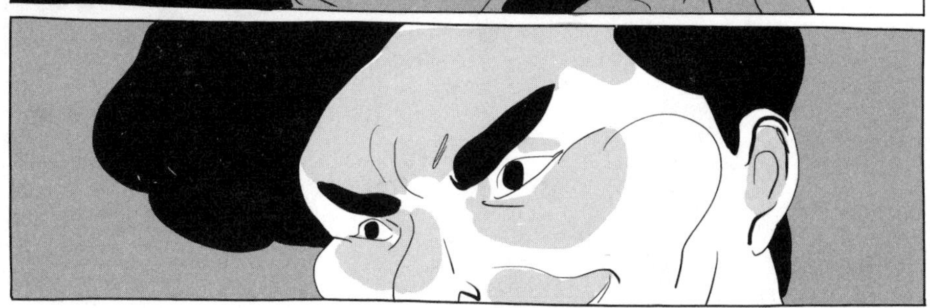

HAI!

TAP
TAK
SLOW DOWN, ADRIAN!
DON'T WASTE YOUR ENERGY!

PANT!
PANT!
PANT!
HAI!
OKAY, FUN'S OVER!
ADRIAN, WATCH OUT!

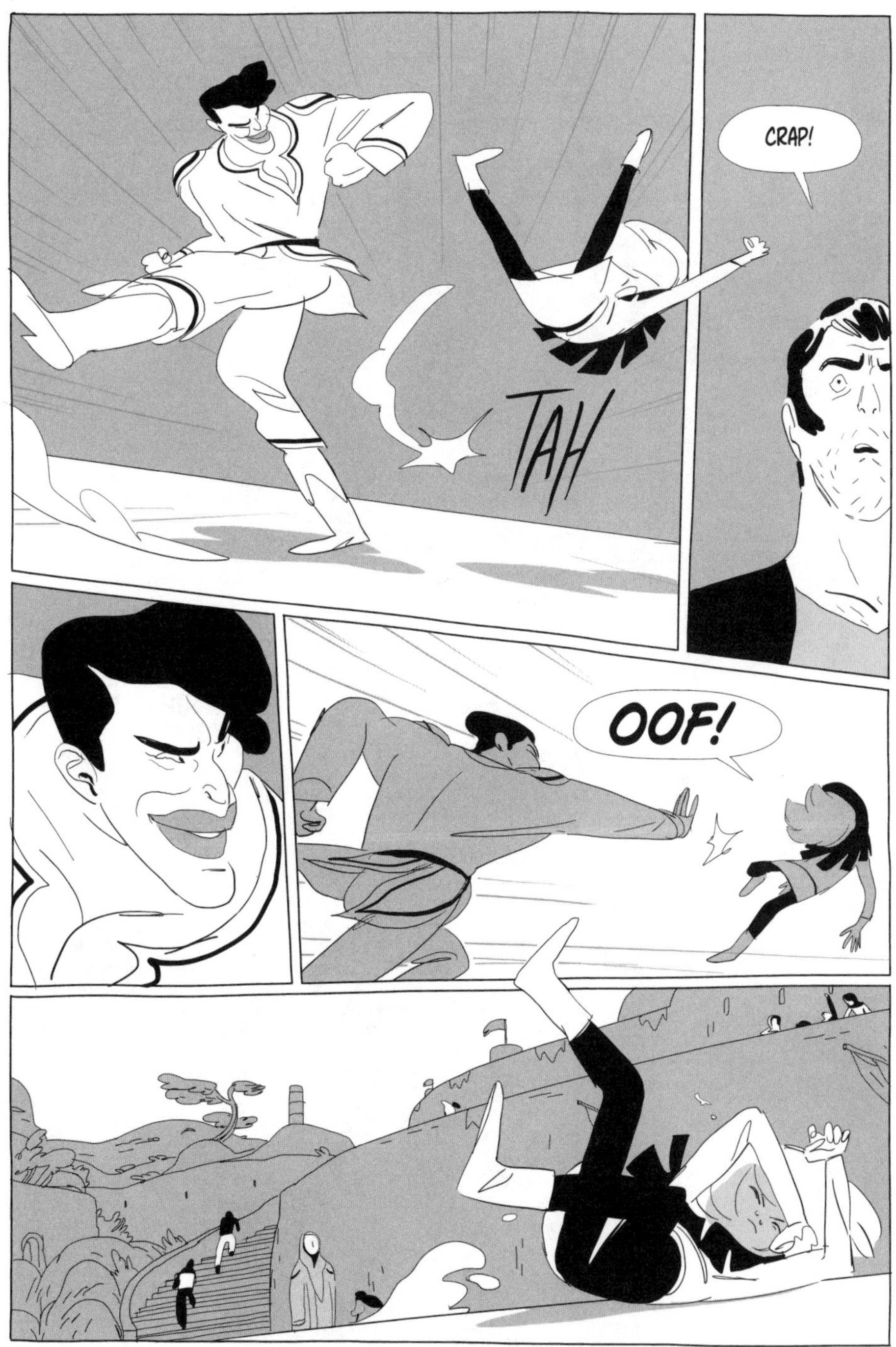
TAH
CRAP!
OOF!

ADRIAN, PUT YOUR GUARD UP...

DAMN IT, ADRIAN! WHAT DO THEY TEACH AT THAT SCHOOL? HOW TO GET YOUR ASS KICKED?

HEY, YOU! DON'T TALK TO MY SON LIKE THAT!

WHAT'RE YOU DOING HERE? DON'T YOU HAVE SOME BREAD TO BAKE OR SOMETHING?
VERY FUNNY, ALDANA! YOU THINK I WOULD LEAVE MY SON ALONE WITH A RUFFIAN?
THE RUFFIAN'S TRYING TO ADVISE HIS PARTNER! I DON'T HAVE TIME TO SUGARCOAT IT!
YOU'RE HILARIOUS! ADRIAN ISN'T ONE OF YOUR DRINKING BUDDIES!

LISTEN, I...
SPLAT
RING OUT!

ADRIAN VELBA...

...ELIMINATED!

HE FLEW OFF LIKE A LITTLE BIRD...
HA HA HA!
HE LOOKED SO BRAVE WITH HIS LITTLE FISTS.
TAP! TAP!
YOU OKAY?
IT'S ALL RIGHT. YOU FOUGHT WELL, SWEETIE.
MMM...
ALL RIGHT...
GUESS I'LL HAVE TO SORT THIS OUT MYSELF.

WELL, WELL... AFTER BABY, IT'S DADDY'S TURN.
HEE HEE...
THE FIGHTERS ARE READY.
DON'T WORRY, I'M NOT ONE TO UNDER-ESTIMATE MY OPPONENTS.
FIGHT!

PREPARE YE TO RECEIVE THIS ATTACK.

I SUMMON...

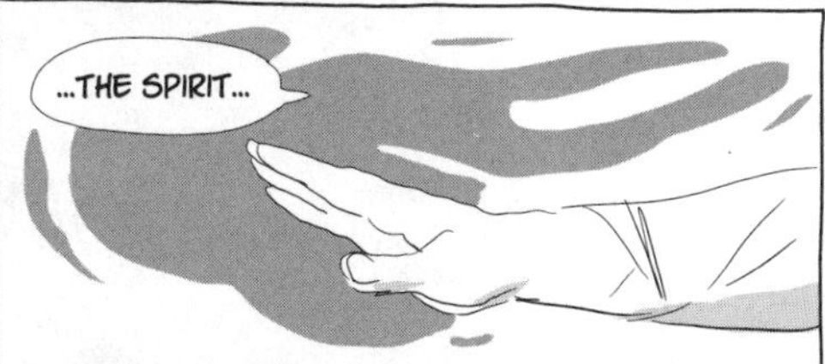
...THE SPIRIT...

THE NORTHERN SCHOOL ATTACK.

...OF THE WIND...

PUT YOUR COAT ON.
MOM...

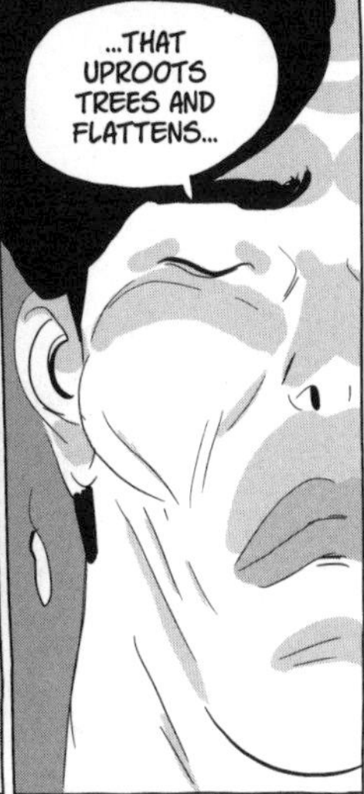
...THAT UPROOTS TREES AND FLATTENS...

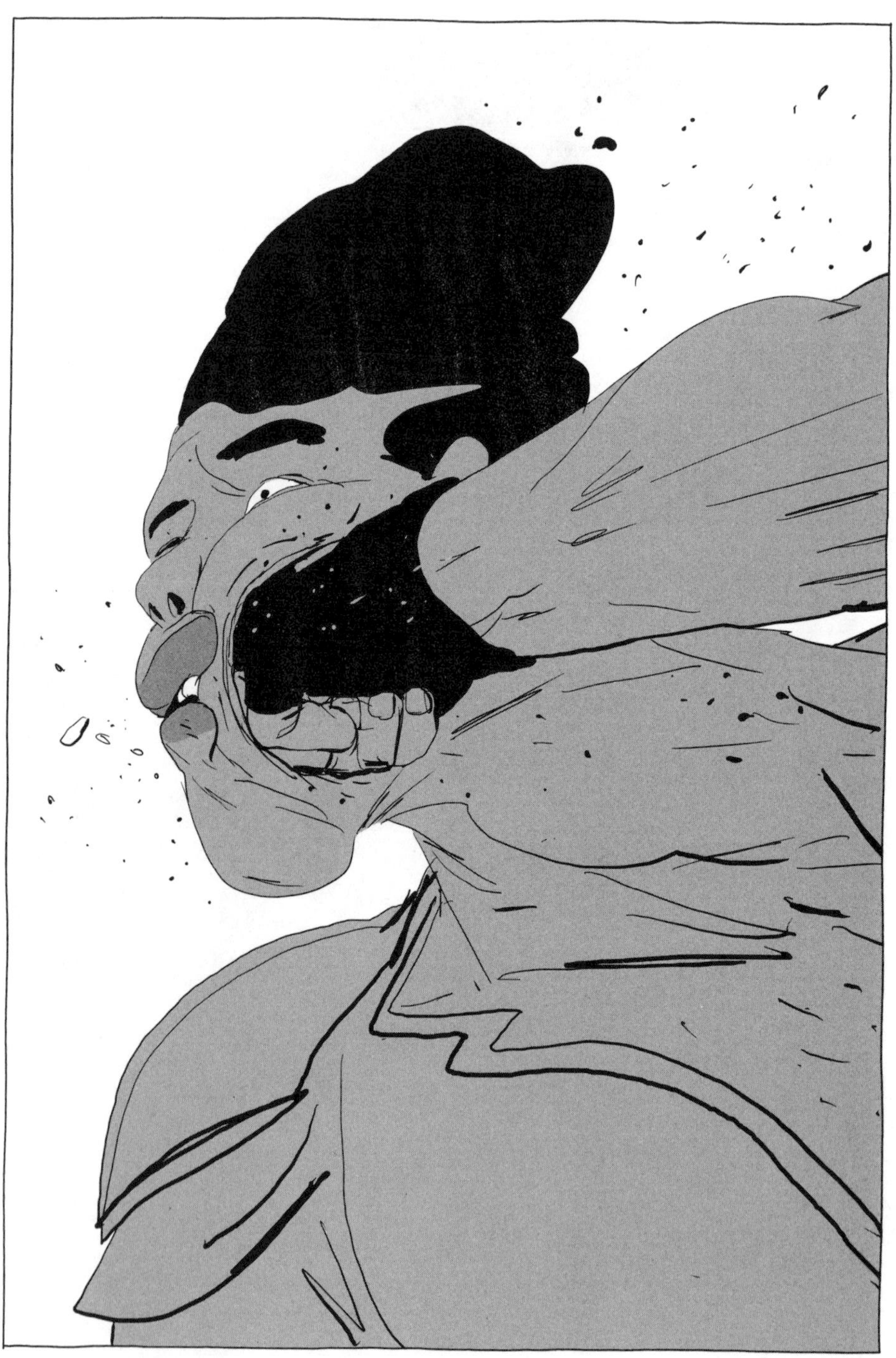

HHHHHH...
NEXT UP! MOVIN' RIGHT ALONG!

PENALTY FOR ENGAGEMENT FOUL.

ALDANA: ONE HAND DOWN.

WHAT?!

IS THAT GUY NUTS?
THIS IS UNHEARD OF!

WHY'D YOU DO THAT?
DO WHAT?
WE'RE NOT ALLOWED TO STRIKE DURING A SUMMONING.

DAMN WEIRD-ASS RULES.

RAMON?
RAMON?
RAMON, CAN YOU HEAR ME?
SPIRIT OF THE LITTLE WIND...
GASP.
ZLA!
OOOH!
OOOH!
WITH...
...ONE BLOW?

YOUR HOLINESS, THIS MAN VIOLATED ALL THE TENETS OF THIS TOURNAMENT.
WHAT SHOULD WE DO?
FIGHTER OF TEAM VELBA-ALDANA...
FOR THIS EGREGIOUS AND DANGEROUS BEHAVIOR WE SHALL GIVE YOU THE HIGHEST PENALTY.
AT THE NEXT STRIKE TAKEN, YOU WILL BE ELIMINATED.

WHAT?
TOO KIND!
I WOULD'VE ELIMINATED
HIM ON THE SPOT!
ALDANA!
IF YOU THINK YOU'LL GET AWAY WITH YOUR DEVIOUS TRICK, THINK AGAIN!
MY BROTHER'S OUT OF THE TOURNAMENT BECAUSE OF YOU!
PREPARE TO GET CRUSHED!
NOW, NOW...

...THOUGHT I TOLD YOU GUYS I'D HAVE YOU BOTH IN A HEAP TODAY.
I REMIND YOU THAT IT IS BLASPHEMOUS TO...
YEAH, YEAH, I GOT IT!

FIGHT!
WHAAAAA

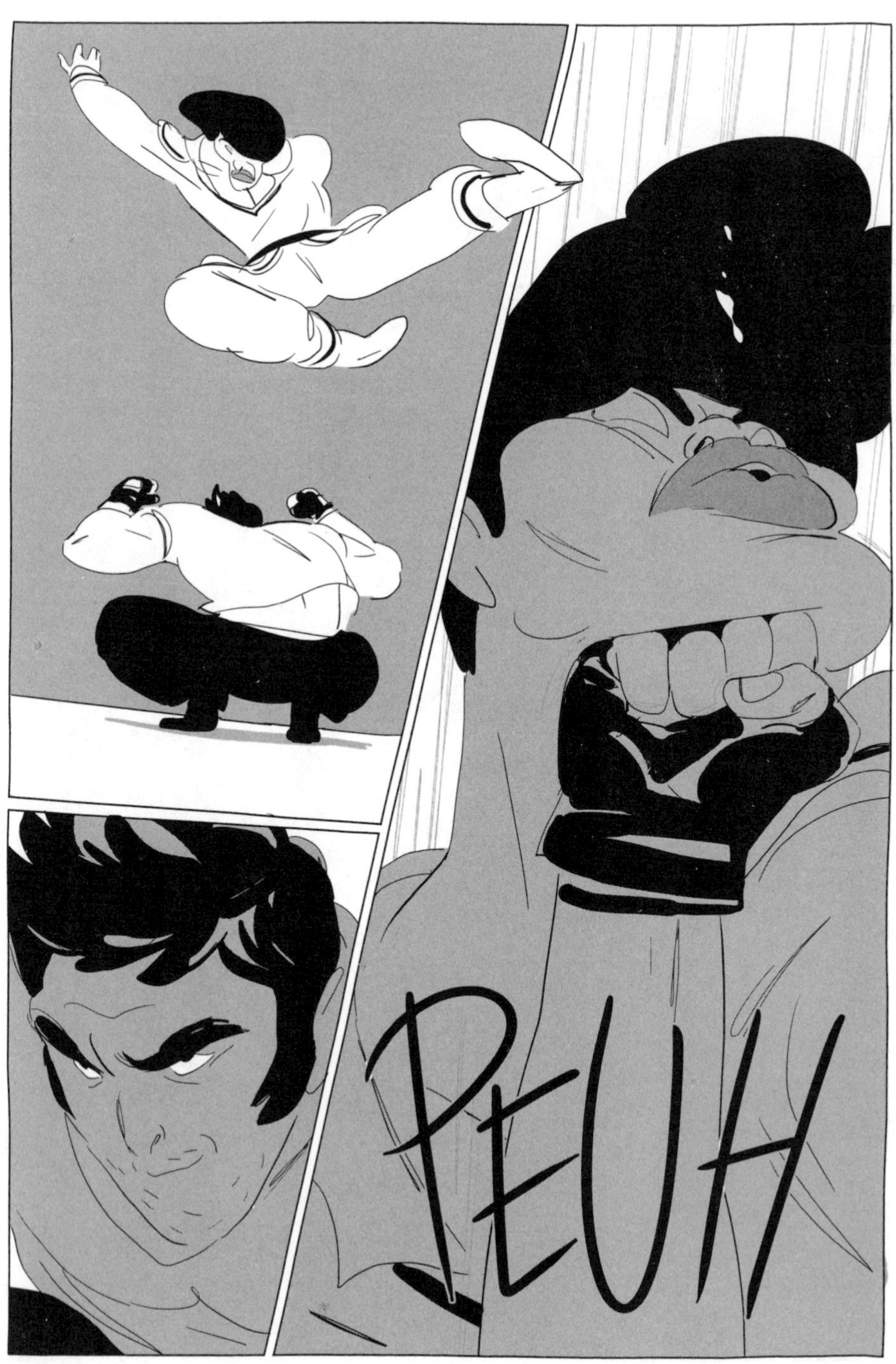
PEUH

OOF!
BLAM!

WHY'RE YOU STOPPING?
WE CAN TAKE A BREAK IF YOU LIKE...
...IF I'M GOING TOO FAST FOR YOU.
BASTARD!

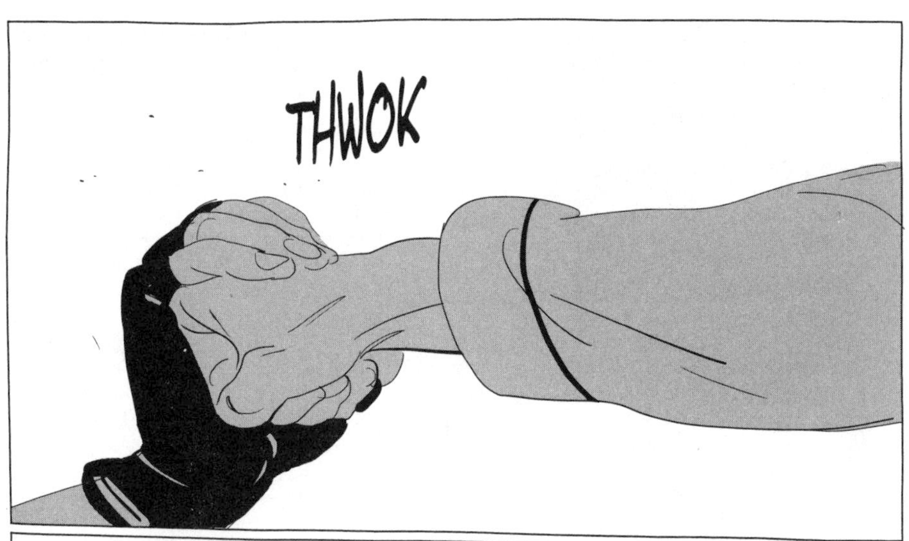
THWOK

SERIOUSLY, DUDE...

WHAT KIND OF DESPERATE ATTACK IS THAT?

SLAP!
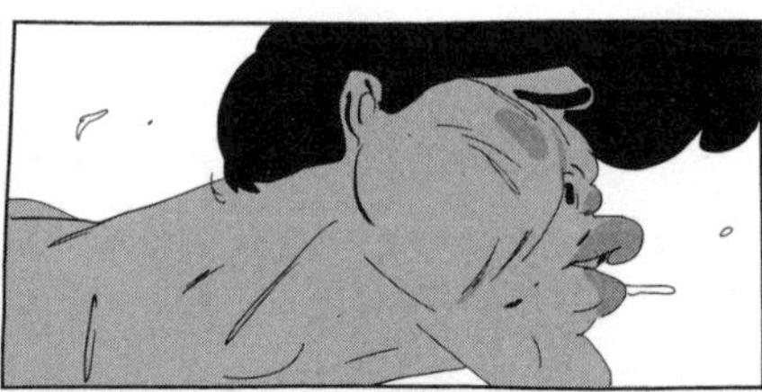

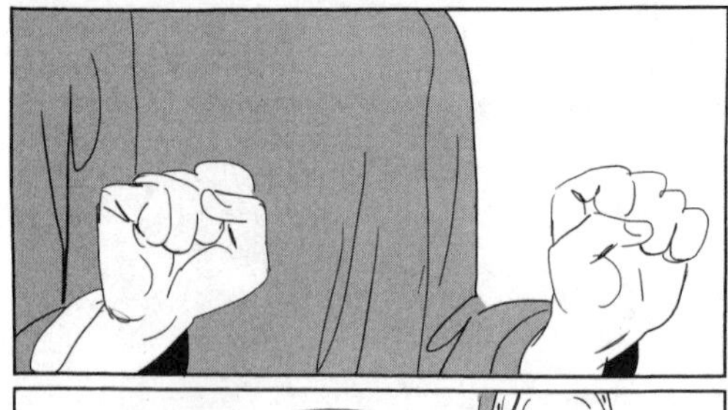

TEAM VELBA-ALDANA QUALIFIES FOR THE SECOND ROUND.

...

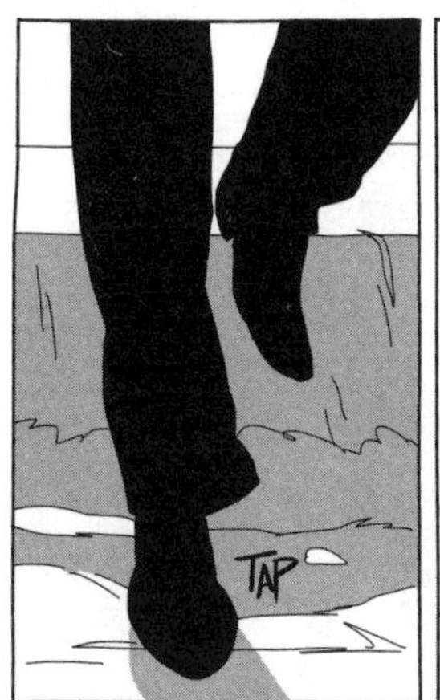
TAP

WOW, RICHARD—
YOU'RE UNBELIEVABLE!

YOU MIGHT'VE LOST, KID, BUT THAT WAS SOME GOOD FIGHTING SPIRIT!

WELL? ENJOY THE SHOW?
YOU CAN HOLD YOUR OWN.

ATTACKING DURING HIS SUMMONING PRAYER...THAT WAS NOBLE.
I'M IMPRESSED.

GOTTA KNOW WHEN TO TAKE RISKS...
IT PAID OFF, DIDN'T IT?

THIS TIME, YES. BUT KEEP YOUR METHODS TO YOURSELF! THAT'S NOT HOW I RAISED ADRIAN.
HIS HAPPINESS IS WHAT MATTERS MOST TO YOU, ISN'T IT?
NOT LOOKING TOO BAD, IS HE?
MY PROMISE STILL STANDS!
ADRIAN IS SAFE WITH ME!
...AND WE'RE GOING TO WIN THIS TOURNAMENT TOGETHER!

COME SEE THE GREATEST FIGHTERS COMPETE IN THE TOURNAMENT!
WHO WILL WIN THE TROPHY THIS YEAR?
SECOND QUALIFYING ROUND!

FIGHT!
MINDANGO WINS!
K.O.!
JASON WINS!
CLOSED HAND! ELIMINATED!
ALYSSA WINS!

ELORNA WINS!

ALDANA WINS!

GREGORIO!

RING OUT!

HEY, MARIANNE! I HEARD YOUR KID'S STILL IN THE RUNNING...

YOU CAN TAKE THE DAY OFF IF YOU WANT!
I'M GOOD, BOSS. ADRIAN'S A BIG BOY!

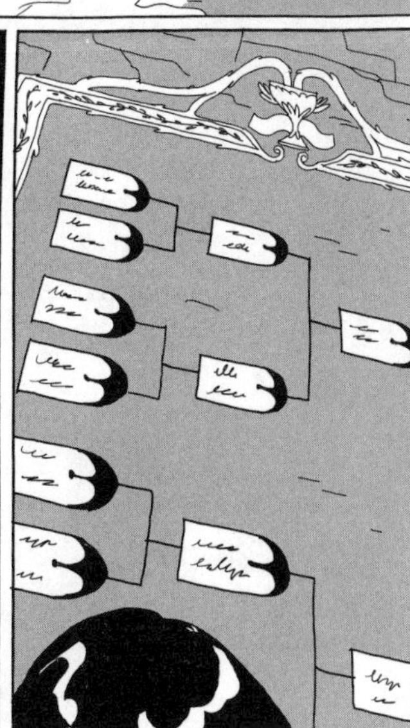

OAK SCHOOL: 2; SOARES BROTHERS: ELIMINATED; MINDANGO: 2-1.
TEAM BRATO-RUBEN. THEY LOST THEIR FIRST TWO FIGHTS. WE SHOULD BE OKAY.
NO, IT'S 2-0. I'M THE ONE WHO BEAT THEM.
SAME DIFFERENCE.
ELORNA!
ARE YOU GONNA BE IN THE QUARTERFINALS?
YEAH, JUST ONE FIGHT TO GO. GREGORIO WAS AMAZING—HE MANAGED TO BEAT GREEM.
CAN YOU BELIEVE IT?
THAT'S RIGHT, MY LITTLE ELORNA. IT SURE WON'T BE YOUR PERFORMANCE THAT GETS US TO THE TO THE QUARTERS.
CUT IT OUT, YOU'RE BEING SILLY. ALL I DID WAS LOSE ONE ROUND.

NO KID HAS EVER GOTTEN PAST THE QUARTERFINALS.
LUCKY FOR YOU, YOUR PARTNER SEEMS TO BE DOING THE WORK.
HE CAN TAKE YOU FAR.
OKAY, OUR NEXT OPPONENTS SEEM MANAGEABLE. THE ONES AFTER THAT ARE TOUGHER.
YOU KNOW CIAMPOLINO AND FILIPPI?
GREAT TEAM. BUT AT THIS POINT IN THE TOURNAMENT, THEY'RE ALL OUTSTANDING.
AND CRISTO CANYON HASN'T ENTERED THE FRAY YET.
CRISTO CANYON?

DOM
DOM

THE REPORT FOR LORD IGNACIO CUDNA.
FOLLOW ME!
SIR, YOUR REPORT.
AH!

PLEASE, COME ON IN!
HOW GOES OUR LITTLE ANNUAL ENTERTAINMENT?
V...VERY WELL, SIR. WE HAVE FIGHTERS—
SNAP!

ELIMINATIONS REPORT... LIKE EVERY YEAR, MINDANGO, URF, JASON, CARMIN, BELA, AND ALYSSA EASILY QUALIFIED!
A FEW SURPRISES: HAY BORELL IS OUT...
TOO OLD!
AS WELL AS MAMBA AND CALIA!
AS ALWAYS, THE SCHOOLS' PERFORMANCE IS ERRATIC. THERE IS, HOWEVER, ONE NOTEWORTHY EXCEPTION...
REALLY?
GREGORIO AND ELORNA OF THE OAK SCHOOL HAVE MADE A STRONG IMPRESSION.
STUDENTS OF THAT NUT JOB JANSEN? THAT SURE IS NEWS!

THAT'S NOT ALL! AN UNKNOWN FIGHTER HAS CAUSED QUITE A STIR...
RICHARD ALDANA.
HE'S THE ONE WHO BEAT MAMBA AND CALIA.
HMM... NEVER HEARD OF HIM.
HE APPARENTLY BEAT ALL HIS OPPONENTS WITHOUT HELP FROM HIS PARTNER, YOUNG ADRIAN VELBA, WHO ISN'T ANY GOOD.
GIVE ME THAT!

PRACTICALLY NO STRIKES TAKEN... ALL KNOCKOUTS, RING OUTS... AND WITHOUT USING ANY SUMMONING AT ALL.

MISS SAKOVA...

I WANT A THOROUGH REPORT ON THIS...

...RICHARD ALDANA.

VICTORY TO TEAM VELBA-ALDANA.
PFF...
I GET THE FEELING THE PUBLIC'S NOT TOO KEEN ON MY STYLE.
TOO DIRECT, I GUESS.
ADRIAN.
YEAH?
ARE YOU SULKING?
HMM...

I HAVEN'T WON A SINGLE ROUND SINCE WE STARTED.
THAT'S NOT SURPRISING. YOU FIGHT LIKE A RAG DOLL.
A RAG DOLL?
INSTEAD OF WORRYING ABOUT WINNING, THERE'S A COUPLE THINGS YOU CAN DO.
FIRST, YOU'RE GONNA STOP COMPLAINING, 'CAUSE IT'S GETTING ON MY NERVES.
SECOND, YOU'RE GONNA GET IT INTO YOUR HEAD THAT WE'RE IN A RING AND NOT A NURSERY.
AND THIRD: I HATE TO SAY IT, BUT YOU'RE 4-FOOT AND 70 POUNDS, SO UP AGAINST GUYS WHO ARE BUILT LIKE BULLS IT'S GONNA BE TOUGH.

BUT IF YOU LISTEN TO ME, I CAN GIVE YOU TWO OR THREE POINTERS THAT'LL HELP YOU OUT.

WE'VE GOT A BIG FIGHT TOMORROW. GET SOME REST, THINK ABOUT WHAT HAPPENED TODAY, AND ALSO...
THINK ABOUT WHY YOU'RE FIGHTING!
WHAT IS IT YOU WANT? WOMEN? MONEY? GLORY? TO BE THE BEST OF THE BEST? THINK ABOUT IT.
ONCE YOU FIND OUT...
THEN, YOU CAN REALLY START FIGHTING.

RICHARD.

WHAT'RE SOME TRICKS FOR FIGHTING BETTER?
I'LL SHOW YOU.

LOOK, THEY'RE OUR NEXT OPPONENTS.

CIAMPOLINO AND FILIPPI.

IF WE BEAT THEM, WE'LL MAKE IT TO THE QUARTERFINALS.

OKAY, SEE YOU TOMORROW.
I WANT YOU WELL RESTED.
WANNA HAVE DINNER AT MY HOUSE?

YOUR HOUSE?
MY MOM SAID I COULD ASK YOU OVER FOR DINNER.

THAT'S NICE OF YOU, ADRIAN, BUT I'D BETTER PREPARE FOR OUR FIGHT TOMORROW. GIVE YOUR MOM A HUG FOR ME.

UGH!
BLAM!

BROUF!

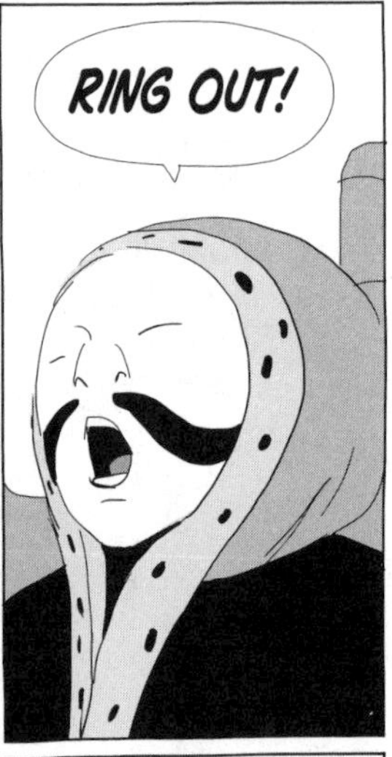
RING OUT!

RICHARD ALDANA WINS!

ADRIAN
VELBA.

RICHARD
ALDANA.

YOU HAVE QUALIFIED FOR THE QUARTERFINALS. MAY THE FIGHTER'S SPIRIT GUIDE YOUR STEPS!

BE DISCERNING AND LET JUSTICE INFORM YOUR EVERY CHOICE.

IT'S AN OUTRAGE! REACHING THE QUARTERFINALS WITH SUCH A CRUDE STYLE!
BAH! YOU GOTTA ADMIT HE'S IMPRESSIVE.

A FIGHTER WHO IS NOT IN SERVICE TO THE ART, TO ITS BEAUTY... BLASPHEMY!

STILL, HIS TECHNIQUE'S PRETTY AMAZING, IN TERMS OF BRUTE FORCE...
YEAH, THAT'S THE WORD! "BRUTE!"
AND NOT A SINGLE DAMN SUMMONING!
A BARBARIAN IN THE QUARTERFINALS! IT'S UNHEARD OF!
THINGS AREN'T WHAT THEY USED TO BE...
GUARD UP, ADRIAN!
GUARD UP!

WATCH— I'LL SHOW YOU.
GO AHEAD; ATTACK ME.
HMMMM...
SHAIIII!
OKAY...
FOR STARTERS, YOU'RE GONNA CUT THAT OUT.
REALLY?
BUT THAT'S THE TREE-SPIRIT SUMMONING!
DON'T GET ME WRONG—TREES ARE GREAT. THEY GROW, THEY GIVE FRUIT, YOU CAN PEE ON THEM, IT'S ALL GOOD. BUT FOR FIGHTING, THEY'RE USELESS.
BUT MASTER JANSEN SAID...

FORGET MASTER JANSEN.
GLOVES HIGH, HEAD TUCKED IN—NOW KEEP YOUR GUARD UP.

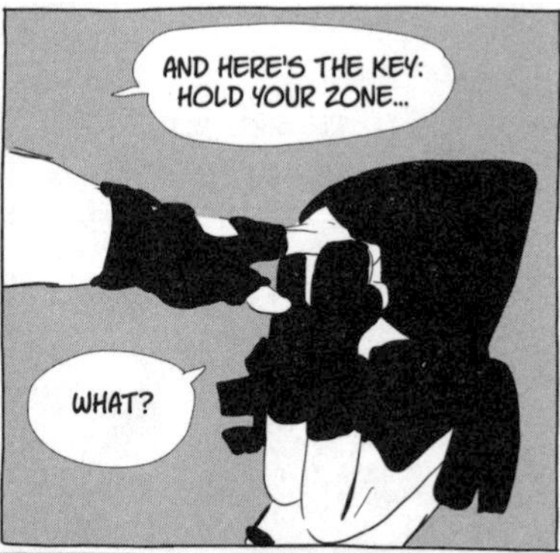
AND HERE'S THE KEY: HOLD YOUR ZONE...
WHAT?

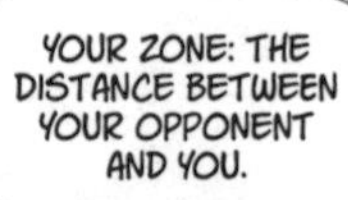
YOUR ZONE: THE DISTANCE BETWEEN YOUR OPPONENT AND YOU.

BUT I CAN'T SEE.

NEVER MIND. JUST LOOK AT MY FEET, AND YOU'LL BE FINE.

THERE, THAT'S IT.

YOUR COMFORT ZONE, ADRIAN—DON'T LET ANYONE IN.

GOOD!

HEY, CHAMPS!
SNACKTIME!

THERE'S
CAKE...

MMMM!

LET GO,
ONI.
GRRRR.
MMM...
SO GOOD!
I'VE NEVER TASTED...
CONGRATULATIONS!
WELL, IT'S
MY JOB...

YES,
BUT STILL...
THIS
IS TRULY
DELICIOUS.

DON'T OVERDO IT, ALDANA.

ONCE YOU'VE WON THAT CUP, YOU'RE HEADING HOME, RIGHT?
AND ANYWAY, I HAVE A QUESTION.
YOU DON'T EXPECT ME TO BELIEVE YOU'RE IN THIS FOR THE JOY OF SPORTSMANSHIP...
DO YOU?
HMM?

HERE WE ARE, SHARING A MOMENT, AND YOU GO SPOIL THE MOOD WITH A CROSS-EXAMINATION...
BUT SINCE IT SEEMS TO BE BOTHERING YOU, WELL...
YES, I COME FROM SOMEWHERE ELSE.
YES, I'M HERE TO WIN THE TOURNAMENT.
AND SINCE IT'S CONFESSION TIME, I HAVE TO ADMIT THAT— OF ALL THE TOURNAMENTS I'VE BEEN IN, THIS ONE'S BY FAR THE MOST PLEASANT.

YOU MIND KEEPING AN EYE ON THE FOOD? I'M GONNA FRESHEN UP AT THE POND.
SURE, NO PROBLEM.

DID YOU BRING YOUR BATHING SUIT?

JUST WATCH THE FOOD, ALDANA.

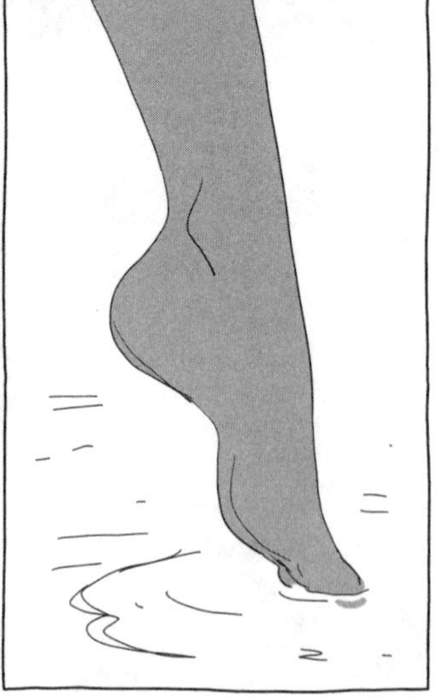

ONI!!!
STOP IT!

BEAT IT!!!

AAAH, I CAN'T BELIEVE IT!

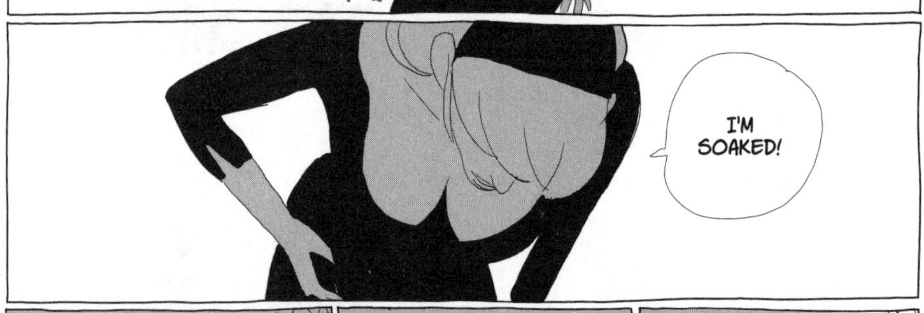
I'M SOAKED!

DAAAAAAMN...

GRRR!!!
WHOA!

GRRRR!!!

IF I UNDERSTAND CORRECTLY, YOU WERE LUCKY TO HAVE THE AFTERNOON OFF.
YES, BUT MY BOSS IS VERY UNDER-STANDING.
CONSIDERING HOW YOU BAKE, HE'D BETTER BE.
TRUE, BUT I'D PREFER BETTER PAY.
DO YOU LIVE OFF TOURNAMENT WINNINGS?
YEAH, PARTLY...
TELL ME, ALDANA.
I WAS WONDERING IF BY ANY CHANCE...
HA HA! ADRIAN, IF YOU THINK I'M IMPRESSED BY YOUR TEAM-MATE...

YOU'VE HAD A NICE RUN, IS ALL.
WHAT'S GOING ON?
WHAT'S GOING ON IS THAT THEY DREW FOR QUARTERFINALS.
IT'S AMAZING YOU EVEN GOT THIS FAR.
WE CAN CONSIDER OURSELVES LUCKY: NEITHER OF US DREW CRISTO CANYON.
BUT THAT MEANS WE'LL ALSO HAVE TO FIGHT ELORNA?
WELL DUH! OBVIOUSLY.
MAYBE MASTER JANSEN HAS SOME ADVICE.
AH!
MASTER JANSEN!
DAMN!

I FORGOT ABOUT THE DINNER!
BUT MOM!

SORRY, RICHARD! SEE YOU SOON!
MOM, LET GO OF ME! I'M NOT A BABY!

I SWEAR, THAT VELBA FAMILY...

MOM!
JUST RUN, ADRIAN!

AHHH!

NICE OUTFIT!
THANK YOU.
UM... YOU TOO!
LEG OF LAMB?
OVER HERE!
SALAD?
YES!
CAREFUL, THE PLATE'S HOT!
THANK YOU.
BON APPÉTIT!
BON APPÉTIT.
SO... HOW'S ADRIAN?

ACTUALLY, I'M A BIT WORRIED ABOUT HIM. YOU SEE EVERYTHING THAT'S HAPPENED IS SO UNUSUAL. HE'S STILL YOUNG AND IT'S NOT EASY TO HANDLE SOMETHING LIKE THAT. AND THIS RICHARD ALDANA IS VERY...ODD.
BUT ADRIAN'S SEEMED MUCH HAPPIER SINCE THEY MET. I GUESS I DON'T KNOW IF I SHOULD BE PLEASED OR ALARMED BY THAT.
WHO WOULD'VE THOUGHT ADRIAN WOULD TAKE A LIKING TO SOMEONE SO...
UM...HOW DO I PUT IT?
ROUGH, YOU KNOW...
YES, "ROUGH"!

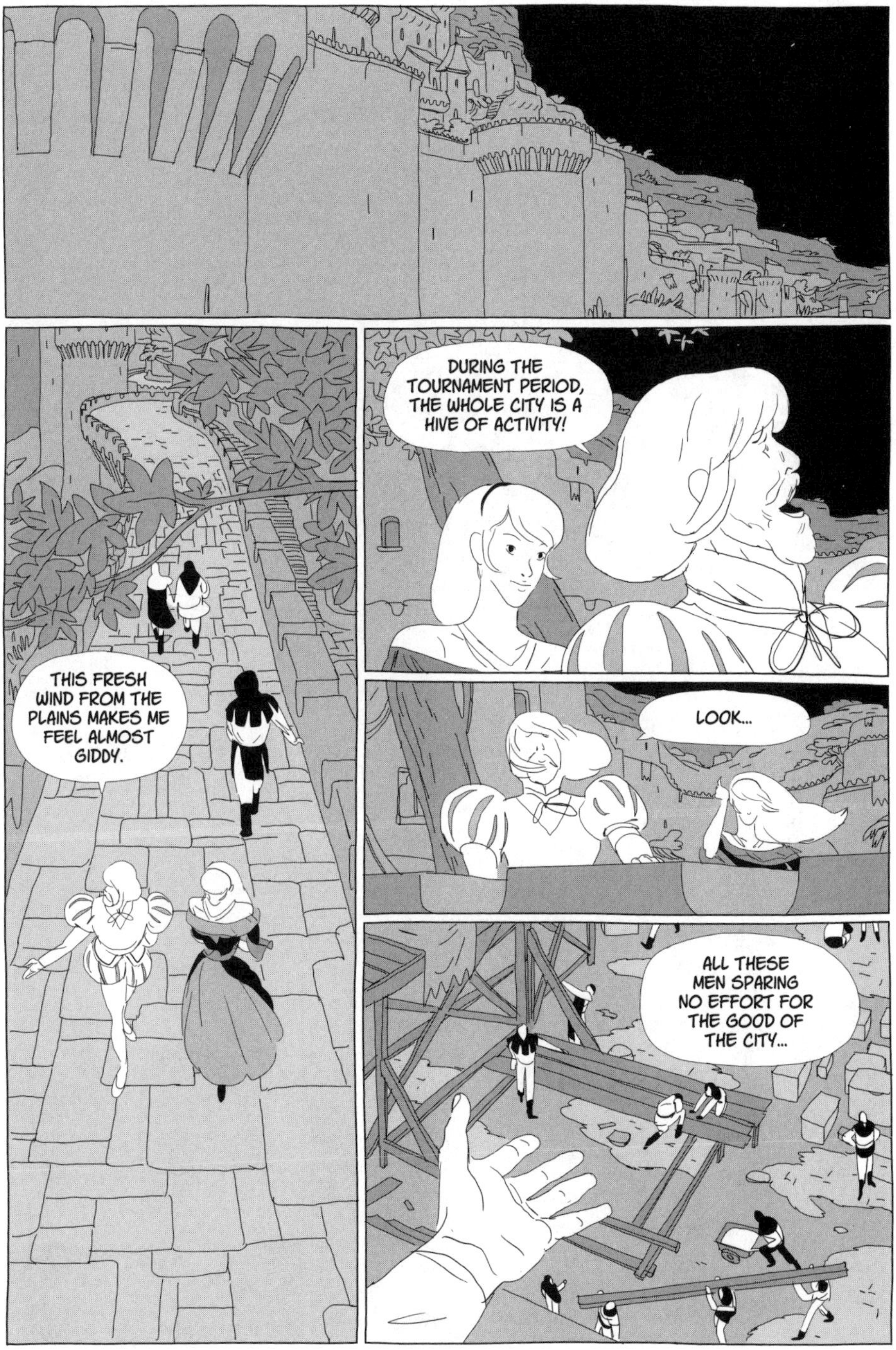

THIS FRESH WIND FROM THE PLAINS MAKES ME FEEL ALMOST GIDDY.

DURING THE TOURNAMENT PERIOD, THE WHOLE CITY IS A HIVE OF ACTIVITY!

LOOK...

ALL THESE MEN SPARING NO EFFORT FOR THE GOOD OF THE CITY...

OUR BEAUTIFUL CITY, SPARKLING LIKE A GEM. ISN'T IT MAGICAL?
YES.
THE STONES THEMSELVE
HEY THERE, LOVEBIRDS!
CHEERS!

MR. ALDANA, IS THIS HOW YOU'RE PREPARING FOR YOUR FIGHT TOMORROW?
HA HA!
THAT'S ONE WAY OF LOOKING AT IT. AND YOU? HOW GOES IT MISS VELBA? NOW I GET WHAT THE HURRY WAS ABOUT, EARLIER...
NICE OUTFIT, MASTER!
SIR, PLEASE TAKE YOUR FEET OFF THE TABLE...
SORRY, BABE!
WHY DON'T YOU SIT ON MY LAP, AND WE'LL TALK THIS OVER!
SIR, THAT'S...
SO WHAT'S YOUR NAME, CUTIE?
STOP IT!

GET YOUR HANDS OFF ME!
LOOKS LIKE WE'RE INTRUDING... LET'S GO, JANSEN!
GOOD NIGHT, ALDANA!

DID YOU SEE THAT? WHAT A PIG! ONCE THIS TOURNAMENT'S OVER, HE WON'T HAVE ANYTHING TO DO WITH ADRIAN!

I SHUDDER TO THINK WHAT IDEAS HE'S BEEN PUTTING IN MY SON'S HEAD!

WELL, HERE WE ARE...
THANKS AGAIN FOR TONIGHT. I HADN'T BEEN OUT TO DINNER IN A LONG TIME.
OR A FAIRLY LONG TIME, AT LEAST.
IT'S JUST...

WELL... I WAS JUST WONDERING IF YOU'D LIKE TO HAVE A DRINK INSIDE...
BUT IF YOU'RE BUSY...

I LOVE YOU!

MARIANNE!
I LOVE YOU...

I...
I...
WHAT?

FROM THE BEGINNING, SINCE THE FIRST DAY YOU CAME TO THE SCHOOL WITH ADRIAN...I SET MY EYES ON YOU, AND MY HEART STOPPED BEATING. I CAN'T SLEEP...

I CAN'T EAT... I DON'T EVEN GO OUT ANYMORE. I JUST STAY HOME DREAMING OF WHEN I'LL SEE YOU AGAIN...

I BEG YOU, MARIANNE, DON'T REJECT ME. IF I COULD JUST...

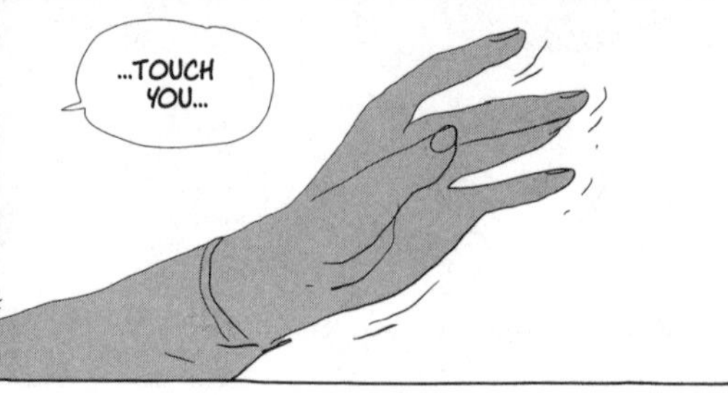
...TOUCH YOU...

MR. JANSEN...

WHAT'S COME OVER YOU?

NO, MARIANNE, DON'T JUDGE ME! I'M DESPERATE!!!

LISTEN, IT'S GETTING LATE. I THINK IT'D BE BETTER IF YOU WENT HOME.

GO HOME?

CALM DOWN?
CALM DOWN?!!
NOT SO LOUD, PLEASE.
I SHOULD CALM DOWN!!!
MR. JANSEN, I BEG YOU...
I SHOULD CALM DOWN!!!

I SHOULD CALM...
...DOWN!!!
BOK!!!
MARIANNE! I'M LOSING MY MIND!!!

YOU DON'T KNOW WHAT YOU'RE SAYING...
AAAAH!!!
YOU DON'T UNDER-STAND.
LOOK, YOU REALLY NEED TO GO BACK TO YOUR—
BOK!
AH...
AH...
AAAH...
MARIANNE...

CLACK!
N...
NO...
MARIANNE...
M...
MARIANNE...

BOM!
PFF...
AAAAA
RGH

MOM?

MOM, IS THAT YOU?

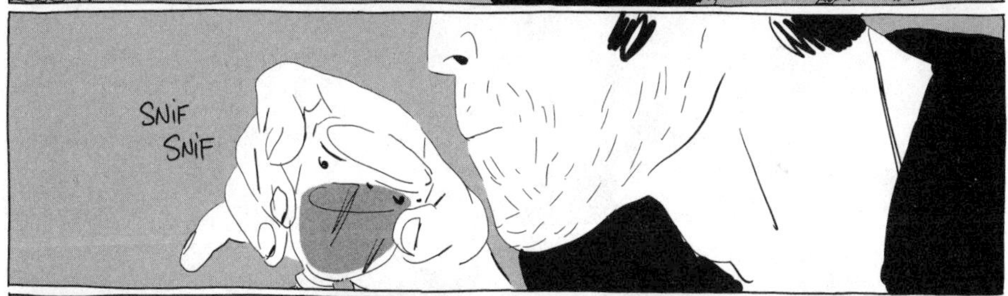
SNIF
SNIF

HEY, WHAT IS THIS CRAP? SMELLS LIKE DRAIN CLEANER.
YOU DID ASK FOR THE STRONGEST LIQUOR IN THE HOUSE. YOU GOT IT.

UGH... THANKS, BUT I'LL HAVE A BEER AFTER ALL.

IS THIS SEAT TAKEN?

MISS VELBA...
IT'S AN HONOR.

NEED A DRINK?
WHAT'RE YOU HAVING?

I DON'T KNOW, AND I THINK I'M BETTER OFF THAT WAY...
MAY I?

SNIF...
SNIF...

UGH... THAT STINKS!
YUCK!

THAT'S WHAT I WAS TELLING YOU...

BUT WHY ARE YOU DRINKING THIS STUFF?
IT'S AWFUL.

WELL, I SWITCHED AND ORDERED A...

HMM...

AHHH...

MMM...

LISTEN, ALDANA.
ADRIAN IS A SENSITIVE BOY.
I KNOW, WE ALREADY TALKED ABOUT IT. I...
NO!

IF YOU
HURT HIM IN
ANY WAY...
IF YOU TRY TO
DECEIVE HIM OR USE HIM...
TRAMPLING ALL
OVER HIS FEELINGS
LIKE SOME SELFISH
BASTARD...
...THERE WON'T BE A
SINGLE PLACE IN THE WORLD
FOR YOU TO HIDE.
I'LL FIND YOU AND
KICK THAT PRETTY LITTLE ASS
OF YOURS. UNDERSTOOD?

I BELIEVE
I GOT THE MESSAGE,
MISS VELBA.
PUNCHY, ISN'T
SHE?
I THINK
IT SUITS
HER.

...AND THE BEER YOU ORDERED.
THANKS.
YOU'RE ALSO PAYING FOR THE LADY'S DRINK, RIGHT?
HERE.
HMM... DON'T KNOW WHERE YOU GOT THIS COIN, BUT IT'S NOT FROM AROUND HERE.
THIS ONE?
NOPE...

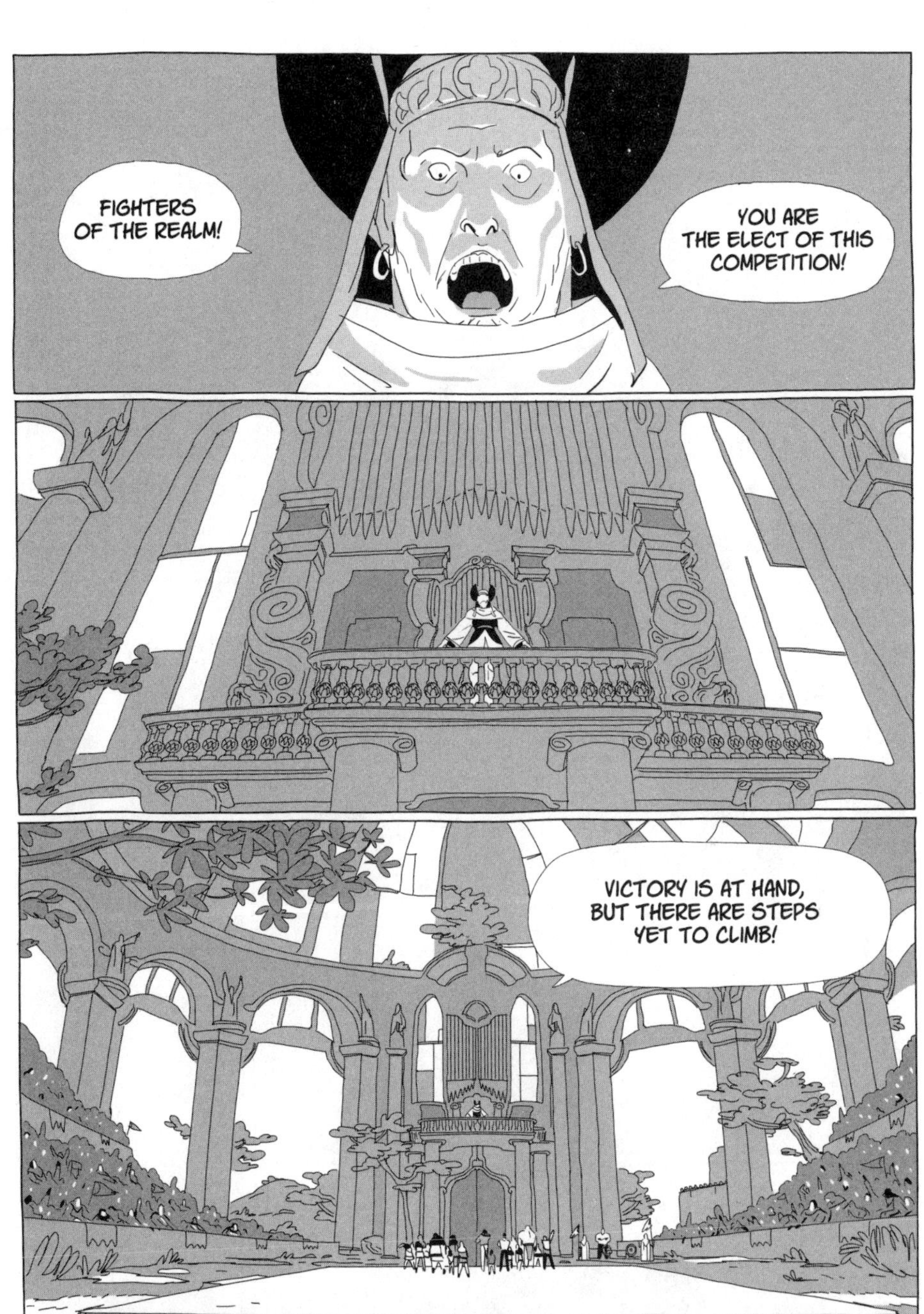
FIGHTERS OF THE REALM!
YOU ARE THE ELECT OF THIS COMPETITION!
VICTORY IS AT HAND, BUT THERE ARE STEPS YET TO CLIMB!

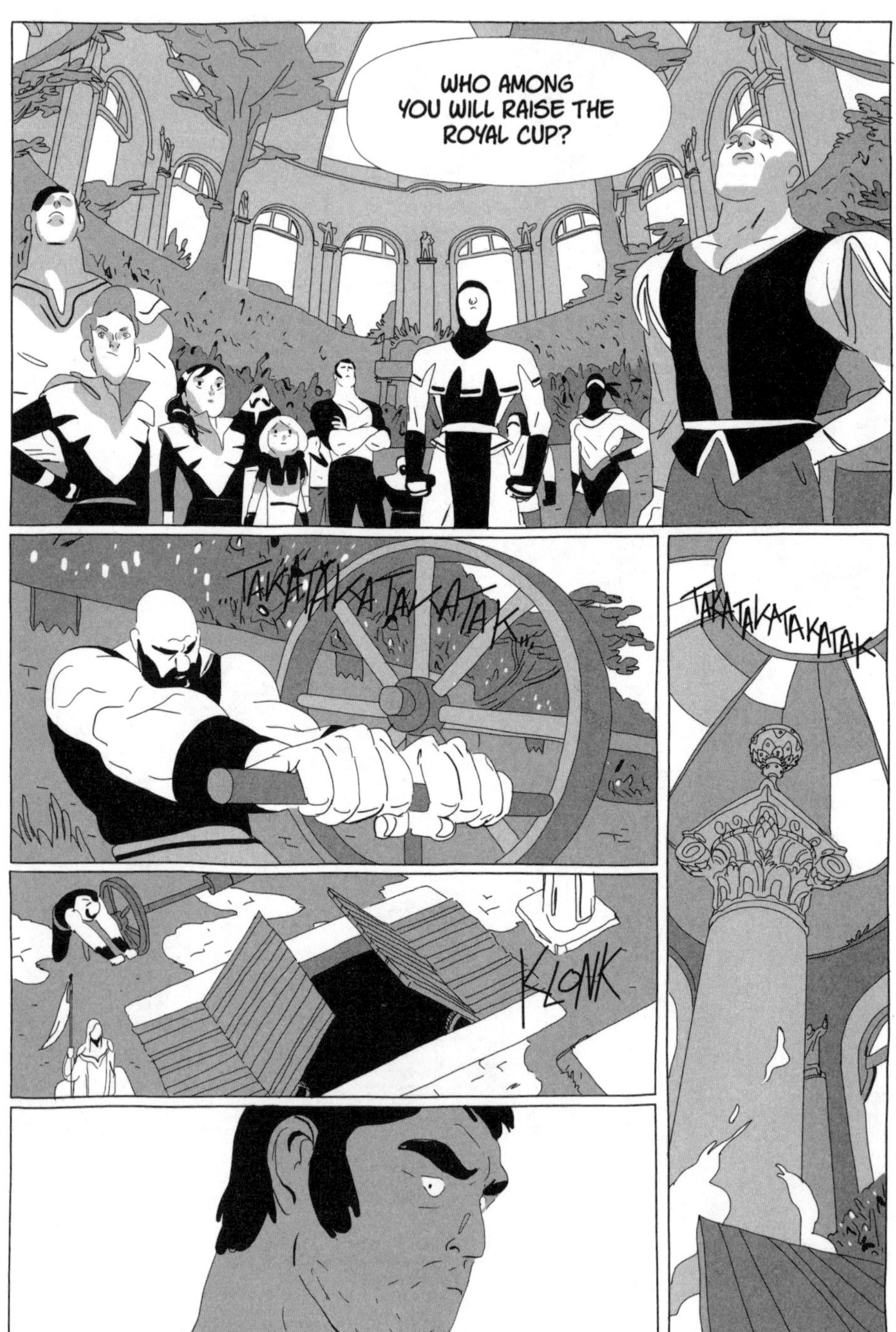
WHO AMONG YOU WILL RAISE THE ROYAL CUP?
TAKATAKATAKATAK
TAKATAKATAKATAK
KLONK

RAAAAAAAAAAAAA
THE ROYAL CUP!
WOOOO!
THE CUP!

ISN'T IT BEAUTIFUL?

I NEVER EVER THOUGHT I'D ACTUALLY SEE IT FROM HERE...

RELAX, ADRIAN!
EASIER SAID THAN DONE!

BWAAAAAAAAAAAAAAAAAAA

PEOPLES OF THE REALM, BRING YOUR HANDS TOGETHER AND SALUTE...

THEIR MAJESTIES
KING VIRGIL AND QUEEN
EFIRA!

BRING IN THE DEFENDING CHAMPIONS.

YAAAAAAAAAHHHH!!!

LORD IGNACIO CUDNA

AND

CRISTO CANYON.

PFFF...

WOW! THAT'S CRISTO CANYON!

THE GREATEST CHAMPION OF ALL TIME!

THE FIRST FIGHT WILL PIT TEAM GREGORIO-ELORNA AGAINST TEAM VELBA-ALDANA!
GO ELORNA!
KIDS FROM OUR SCHOOL FINALLY MAKE IT TO THE QUARTER FINALS... AND THEY HAVE TO FIGHT EACH OTHER. THAT SUCKS.
WHAT DO YOU THINK, MASTER?

MASTER?

HMM...
YES, INDEED, IT'S UNFORTUNATE.
REGRETTABLY FOR ADRIAN, THERE IS NO DOUBT AS TO THE OUTCOME.

BUT RICHARD ALDANA SEEMS SO POWERFUL.

HEE HEE!
HE WON'T IF GREGORIO FOLLOWS MY INSTRUCTIONS EXACTLY!

FIGHTER
GREGORIO!

FIGHTER
ALDANA!

PREPARE TO
ENGAGE!

LISTEN CAREFULLY, GREGORIO. IF YOU WANT TO BEAT THAT THUG ALDANA...
...THERE IS A SUBTLE STRATEGY THAT I'VE DEVELOPED...
FIGHT!
UPON ENGAGEMENT, MOVE BACK AS QUICKLY AS POSSIBLE.
SHHHH
GROUND YOURSELF IN YOUR STANCE, SUMMON THE SPIRITS...
TAP
...AND THEN...
LET IT FLY!

WAM WAM
VOLLEY!!!
WAM
BLOC!
BLOC!
WOOSH
C'MON, KIDDO. GET OVER HERE...
KEEP YOUR POSTURE AND LET HIM HAVE IT.
WAM

STOP HIM FROM MOVING FORWARD...
PAK
AIM AT EYE LEVEL.
SHHH
WAM
WAM
WHAT THE—
SHHH
NOW.

THUNDER!!!
!
WAM!
WH...
RICHARD!

YAAAAH!!!
HEY, WHAT THE HELL IS THIS?!!!
WILL YOU CUT THE CRAP?!
VOLLEY!!!
WAM
WAM
OKAY, IF THAT'S HOW YOU WANT IT!
SHHA-

AIM FOR THE EYES...
TAP
BLAST AWAY!
QUICKLY REGAIN YOUR DISTANCE.
ENOUGH OF THIS SH-
RICHARD, WATCH OUT! YOUR GUARD!
KEEP CLEAR...
...LET RIP...
DISTANCE, DISTANCE...

VOLLEY!
WAM
COME AND FIGHT!

YOU HAVING FUN? I DON'T FEEL A THING!
KSHH
KSHH
KSHH
KEEP GOING—SEE IF I CARE!

RICHARD, DON'T!

NO, NO, NO!

RICHARD ALDANA...
...ELIMINATED!

WH...
YOU SEE, GREGORIO...
ALDANA'S NOT BAD...
...BUT HE'S A THUG... FOR EVERY FIGHT...
...HE'S WON BY KNOCKOUTS AND RING OUTS...
YOUR ATTACKS WOULD'VE HAD NO EFFECT...
...SO WE'RE GOING TO GIVE HIM A LESSON IN COMBAT...
...THAT HE'LL HAVE PLENTY OF TIME TO THINK ABOUT.

CLAP!
CLAP!
YOU KNOW WHAT? I'M GOING INTO THE RING TO AVENGE YOU!
RICHARD...
DON'T MAKE ME LAUGH, ADRIAN.
R...
MORON...

SO THAT'S THE FEARSOME ALDANA? A FOOL WHO FALLS HEADLONG INTO A BEGINNER'S TRAP?
HEY, ADRIAN!
READY FOR A LITTLE REPEAT OF OUR TRAINING SESSION?
HMM?

Read on for a preview of

LAST MAN

2

The Royal Cup

Balak + Sanlaville + Vivès

Available in June 2015 by First Second Books

ISBN 978-1-62672-047-3

YOU'RE A WEAKLING, ADRIAN!
HA HA!
YOU THINK I DON'T NOTICE YOU'RE GREEN WITH ENVY...
...WHEN YOU WATCH ME TRAIN
YOU THINK I DON'T SEE...
...HOW YOU LOOK AT ELORNA?
NO HARM IN DREAMING.
BUT YOU'RE GONNA HAVE TO REALIZE...
...YOU'RE NOTHING MORE THAN A LITTLE KID.

QUAKE!
BRAAA!!!

BUT...
BUT...
OOH!
WHAT?
THAT'S PRACTICALLY ONE HAND!!
...ADRIAN...
!!!
WHAT THE...
ADRIAN!

New York

Published by First Second
First Second is an imprint of Roaring Brook Press,
a division of Holtzbrinck Publishing Holdings Limited Partnership
175 Fifth Avenue, New York, New York 10010

Cataloging-in-Publication Data is on file at the Library of Congress

ISBN: 978-1-62672-046-6

First Second books may be purchased for business or promotional use. For information on bulk purchases please contact Macmillan Corporate and Premium Sales Department at (800) 221-7945 x5442 or by email at specialmarkets@macmillan.com.

Originally published in France by Casterman as *Lastman tome 1*.

First American edition 2015

Cover design by Colleen AF Venable
Book design by Rob Steen

Printed in the United States of America

10 9 8 7 6 5 4 3 2 1